Printed in the United States of America.

Springer Literary House LLC
6260 Lavender Cloud Place
Las Vegas, Nevada 89122, USA
www.springerliteraryhouse.com

# HUMANITY'S COMPASS:
# NAVIGATING LIFE IN THE DIGITAL AGE

**RAY SMITH**

# PREFACE

In an era defined by rapid technological advancement and digital connectivity, we find ourselves navigating a complex landscape that influences every aspect of our lives. We are no longer simply inhabitants of a physical world; we are also citizens of the digital realm, navigating a vast and ever-evolving sea of information. This signifies the emergence of a newly created universe I called the "**Digiverse**", a world that is imaginary yet has a profound impact on our daily lives.

*Humanity's Compass: Navigating Life in the Digital Age* is a reflection on this new reality—a guide designed to help readers navigate the myriad challenges and a call to embrace opportunities that arise in the digital world.

As the author, I have witnessed firsthand how technology shapes our interactions, our communities, and our understanding of ourselves.

While the digital age offers remarkable tools for communication, learning, and creativity, it also presents profound ethical dilemmas and challenges to our humanity. This book aims to explore those complexities, encouraging readers to critically examine their relationship with technology and its impact on their lives.

**Humanity's Compass** invites you to reflect on the ways technology can enhance our lives while also urging us to remain grounded in our values, wisdom, and moral compass. My hope is that this book will serve as a resource for anyone seeking to cultivate a balanced and meaningful existence in a world increasingly dominated by screens and algorithms.

Throughout the chapters that follow, we'll explore deeper into crucial topics such as digital empathy, online ethics, and the irreplaceable value of face-to-face connections. Through engaging stories, practical advice, and thought-provoking exercises, you'll be encouraged to reflect on your own experiences and make conscious choices about how you interact with technology and others. This journey is not about rejecting the digital world, but rather about learning to harness its benefits while staying true to your human essence.

As we progress through this book, the author will equip you with the tools and insights needed to create a more compassionate, balanced, and fulfilling life in the digital age. You'll learn how to cultivate meaningful relationships, both online and offline, and how to use technology as a force for good in your personal life and in society. By the end of our journey, you'll have developed your own 'humanity's compass' – a personalized guide to help you navigate the complexities of the digital world while nurturing the timeless values that make us human.

Thank you for joining me on this exploration. May this book provide you with the insights and guidance you need to chart your own course in the digital world.

# ACKNOWLEDGMENT

Writing **Humanity's Compass: Navigating Life in the Digital Age** has been an extraordinary journey, and I am deeply grateful to everyone who played a role in bringing this book to life.

First, my heartfelt thanks to my family and friends for their unwavering support and encouragement. Your belief in me has been a constant source of strength and inspiration. I am also immensely grateful to my fellow book authors and colleagues, whose insights and guidance helped shape my vision for this book and refine its message.

Secondly, a big thanks to Springer Literary House, who is not only my publisher but have also been incredibly supportive at every step until I finished the book.

To my co-writer who wishes to be remain in the shadow of anonymity but whose contribution as pivotal, and at the same time my mentor in writing, Rey Sanosa—without you, I could not have written and finish this book.

To the readers navigating this digital age alongside me, thank you for your curiosity and commitment to understanding our evolving world. This book is for you, and it is my hope that it serves as a compass to help you thrive in a rapidly changing landscape.

Lastly, to everyone who assisted in the writing, editing, and publishing of **Humanity's Compass**, I extend my deepest appreciation. Your hard work and dedication have made this book possible, and I am truly grateful.

# SYNOPSIS

In *"Humanity's Compass: Navigating Life in the Digital Age,"* Ray Smith offers a compelling roadmap for young people seeking to maintain their humanity in an increasingly digital world. This thought-provoking book addresses the challenges faced by teenagers and young adults as they grapple with the influence of technology on their lives, relationships, and values. Through a series of engaging stories, practical advice, and thought-provoking concepts, Smith encourages readers to reflect on their own experiences and make conscious choices about how they interact with technology and others. The book explores themes such as digital empathy, online ethics, and the importance of face-to-face connections. By emphasizing the value of each human life, promoting respect, and nurturing timeless values, *"Humanity's Compass"* empowers young readers to harness the benefits of technology while staying true to their human essence. This essential guide inspires a new generation to create a more compassionate, balanced, and fulfilling world both online and offline.

# TABLE OF CONTENTS

CHAPTER 1
**Introduction: The Digital Dilemma**     15

CHAPTER 2
**Digital Empathy: Connecting Hearts**     29
**Through Screens**

CHAPTER 3
**Online Ethics: Navigating the Virtual**     39
**Moral Landscape**

CHAPTER 4
**The Power of Face-to-Face Connections**     61

CHAPTER 5
**Harnessing Technology**     75
**for Personal Growth**

CHAPTER 6
**Charting Your Course:**     85
**Creating A Balanced Digital Life**

CHAPTER 7
**The Future with Ai: Shaping the World of**     95
**Tomorrow**

# CHAPTER 1

# INTRODUCTION: THE DIGITAL DILEMMA

# The Digital Dilemma

The digital world, while offering immense opportunities, presents a growing list of problems. The spread of misinformation and disinformation has become rampant, eroding trust and fueling societal divisions. Cybersecurity threats are escalating, compromising personal data and jeopardizing national security. Social media platforms, designed for connection, often breed negativity, anxiety, and a distorted perception of reality. Addiction to technology is on the rise, impacting mental health and disrupting real-world relationships. The digital divide continues to widen, exacerbating inequalities and limiting access to opportunities. These problems demand urgent attention, requiring a collective effort to create a digital landscape that is safe, equitable, and conducive to human well-being.

## 1. The Power of Digital Connectivity

The rise of the internet, social media, and mobile technology has made the world more interconnected than ever before. Information is now at our fingertips, and communication happens in real-time, across vast distances. Digital platforms enable us to share ideas, build communities, and even shape societal movements. In many ways, these advances have brought people closer, allowing individuals to form relationships, access educational resources, and stay informed on global issues from the comfort of their homes. The digital world has also given voice to marginalized groups, offering opportunities for expression and connection that would otherwise be out of reach.

However, this sense of interconnectedness can also breed isolation. The digital space, with its constant bombardment of information and distractions, can leave us feeling disconnected from the real world and the people around us. Social media, for example, often promotes an idealized image of life, creating unrealistic expectations and amplifying feelings of inadequacy, loneliness, and anxiety. In this digital landscape, the lines between connection and alienation are often blurred.

## 2. Privacy vs. Convenience

One of the most pressing issues in the digital age is the tension between privacy and convenience. In exchange for the convenience of personalized services, instant communication, and free access to information, we often sacrifice our personal data. The rise of data-driven algorithms, targeted advertising, and surveillance practices by governments and corporations has raised serious concerns about the extent to which our personal information is being collected, stored, and used. Many individuals unknowingly give up their privacy as they freely share personal details online—be it through social media, search engines, or even online shopping.

This trade-off poses a significant moral and ethical dilemma: How much personal information are we willing to surrender for the sake of convenience, and at what cost to our individual freedoms? In a world where data is currency, the digital dilemma forces us to question who controls our information, how it's used, and whether we are truly in control of our digital identities.

## 3. The Impact on Human Relationships

The digital age has also transformed how we relate to one another. While technology offers endless opportunities for connection, it also has the potential to erode genuine human interaction. The rise of online communication and social networking can sometimes result in a lack of face-to-face interactions, which are critical for developing deeper emotional bonds. In many ways, digital communication lacks the nuance, empathy, and authenticity that in-person conversations offer.

Moreover, the constant connectivity of smartphones and social media platforms means that we are rarely truly "disconnected." This perpetual state of being available, coupled with the pressure to maintain a polished online presence, can create a sense of burnout, anxiety, and detachment from reality. The digital dilemma, in this sense, highlights the challenge of maintaining meaningful relationships while navigating a world that is constantly online.

## 4. Ethical and Societal Concerns

The digital dilemma extends beyond privacy and relationships into broader societal issues. The rise of artificial intelligence (Ai), automation, and robotics has begun to disrupt traditional industries and job markets. While Ai holds tremendous potential for innovation, it also poses significant questions about the future of work and human autonomy. Will Ai replace human jobs, or can it enhance human potential? How can we ensure that technological advancements are used ethically, without reinforcing existing biases or exacerbating inequality?

In addition, the spread of misinformation and "fake news" on digital platforms poses serious threats to democratic processes, public trust, and the stability of societies. The rapid spread of false or misleading information, often fueled by algorithms that prioritize engagement over truth, has made it increasingly difficult to discern fact from fiction in the digital world. This presents a moral dilemma for individuals, media organizations, and governments: How can we balance free speech with the responsibility to protect the integrity of information and prevent harm?

## 5. Finding Balance in the Digital Dilemma

The digital dilemma doesn't have a one-size-fits-all solution. It requires thoughtful reflection, ethical consideration, and a balance between embracing the benefits of technology and safeguarding the values that define us as human beings. We must be intentional in how we use digital tools, ensuring they serve to enrich our lives rather than diminish our well-being.

Education and digital literacy are essential in navigating the complexities of the digital world. By understanding the risks and responsibilities of digital engagement, individuals can make informed decisions and protect their privacy, mental health, and relationships. At the same time, society must work toward creating ethical guidelines and policies that regulate the use of technology, ensuring that digital innovation serves the common good without compromising individual rights.

# The Technological Revolution and Its Impact on Youth

The technological revolution of the 21st century has ushered in an era of unprecedented connectivity and digital innovation, profoundly impacting the lives of young people around the globe. For teenagers and young adults between the ages of 15 and 30, this digital landscape has become an integral part of their daily existence, shaping how they communicate, learn, and perceive the world around them. From smartphones and social media to artificial intelligence and virtual reality, the rapid advancement of technology has created both exciting opportunities and unique challenges for today's youth.

As digital natives, young people have grown up immersed in a world where the lines between online and offline experiences are increasingly blurred. This constant connectivity has revolutionized access to information, expanded social networks beyond geographical boundaries, and opened up new avenues for creativity and self-expression. However, it has also given rise to concerns about digital addiction, cyberbullying, privacy issues, and the potential erosion of face-to-face social skills. The impact of technology on youth mental health, identity formation, and overall well-being has become a topic of intense scrutiny and debate among researchers, educators, and parents alike.

The technological revolution has both positive and negative impacts on everyone's life. Three main factors stand out as transformative for younger generations, offering immense potential yet posing significant risks if misused:

**1. The Information Superhighway:** The internet has become the information superhighway, connecting billions of people around the world. It's a source of knowledge, entertainment, and connection. However, it also enables the rapid spread of misinformation, which can mislead and harm society.

**2. Social Media:** Social media platforms have become a powerful force in the lives of today's young generations lives, shaping their opinions, influencing their decisions, and connecting them with people from all over the world. Despite these benefits, they can also lead to anxiety, unhealthy comparisons, and distractions from real-world interactions and goals.

**3. The Rise of Ai:** Artificial intelligence is rapidly transforming our world, automating tasks, creating new technologies, and changing the way we live, work, and interact with each other. Yet, it raises critical ethical concerns, including issues of privacy, bias, and the implications for the future of work.

Navigating this digital terrain requires a delicate balance between embracing the benefits of technology and maintaining one's humanity. Young people today face the challenge of cultivating meaningful relationships, developing empathy, and nurturing their own values in an environment that often prioritizes virtual connections and instant gratification. As we delve deeper into the digital age, it becomes increasingly crucial for youth to develop a strong moral compass and critical thinking skills to guide them through the complexities of the online world while staying true to their human essence.

## The Need for a Moral Compass in the Digital Age

In today's digital landscape, where information flows freely and technology permeates every aspect of our lives, the need for a moral compass has never been more crucial. Young people, in particular, find themselves navigating a complex web of online interactions, social media pressures, and digital dilemmas that challenge their values and ethical foundations. As we plunge deeper into the digital age, it becomes increasingly important to cultivate a strong sense of right and wrong that can guide us through the murky waters of the internet and beyond.

The digital world, with its vast opportunities and issues, often blurs the lines between what is acceptable and what is harmful. From cyberbullying and online harassment to the spread of misinformation and the addictive nature of social media, teenagers and young adults face a myriad of ethical challenges that previous generations never encountered. A well-calibrated moral compass serves as an essential tool for making sound decisions in this digital landscape, helping young people maintain their integrity, empathy, and human connections in a world that can sometimes feel devoid of these qualities.

Developing a moral compass in the digital age requires a combination of self-reflection, critical thinking, and a commitment to timeless values such as empathy, respect, and honesty. By consciously examining our online behaviors and their impact on others, we can begin to align our digital actions with our core values. This process of introspection and ethical decision-making not only benefits individuals but also contributes to creating a more compassionate and responsible digital community. As we move forward in this chapter, we'll explore practical strategies for cultivating and strengthening your moral compass, ensuring that you can navigate the digital world with confidence, integrity, and a deep sense of humanity.

As mention earlier, to navigate the digital world effectively requires a moral compass which means—a set of guiding principles to help you stay grounded, make informed decisions, and avoid potential risks. By practicing these principles, you can cultivate a mindset rooted in moral and responsible practices:

**1. Critical Thinking**: In a world of information overload, it's more important than ever to be a critical thinker. Question everything, evaluate sources, and don't blindly accept everything you read or hear.

**2. Digital Literacy:** Develop your digital literacy skills. Learn how to use technology effectively, how to protect your privacy, and how to navigate the online world safely.

**3. Balance and Moderation:** The digital world can be addictive. Set boundaries, take breaks, and prioritize real-life experiences over virtual ones.

**4. Ethical Considerations:** Be mindful of the ethical implications of your online actions. Think before you post, be respectful of others, and avoid spreading misinformation.

# CHAPTER 2

# DIGITAL EMPATHY: CONNECTING HEARTS THROUGH SCREENS

## Connecting Hearts Through Screens

In a world increasingly dominated by screens, a new kind of intimacy has emerged: connecting hearts through pixels. While physical distance may separate us, the digital realm allows us to bridge the gap, sharing laughter, tears, and dreams through virtual windows. It's a testament to the human spirit's resilience, finding connection in the face of isolation, forging bonds that transcend geographical boundaries. The warmth of a virtual hug, the comfort of a late-night chat, the shared joy of a digital celebration – these are the threads that weave a tapestry of connection, reminding us that even in the digital age, human connection remains the most powerful force of all.

The screen, once a barrier, has become a bridge. It allows us to connect with loved ones across continents, share our passions with like-minded individuals, and find solace in the virtual embrace of a community. We laugh together, cry together, and celebrate life's milestones, all through the magic of the digital world. This is the power of connecting hearts through screens — a testament to the human spirit's ability to adapt, connect, and find meaning in an ever-evolving world.

## Understanding Emotions in the Digital Space

In the digital age, understanding emotions has taken on a new dimension. As we increasingly communicate through screens, the challenge of interpreting and conveying feelings without the benefit of facial expressions or tone of voice has become more pronounced. This digital emotional landscape requires a new set of skills, ones that combine traditional empathy with an understanding of how emotions are expressed and perceived in online spaces.

For young people navigating this digital terrain, it's crucial to develop a keen awareness of how words, emojis, and even the timing of messages can impact emotional understanding.

The absence of physical cues can lead to misinterpretations, making it essential to practice clarity in digital communication. By honing these skills, we can bridge the gap between our offline emotional intelligence and our online interactions, fostering deeper connections even through the barrier of screens.

Moreover, recognizing the emotional impact of our digital footprint is vital. Every post, comment, or reaction we leave online has the potential to affect others emotionally. As we cultivate digital empathy, we must consider not only how we express our own emotions but also how our online actions might influence the emotional well-being of others. This heightened awareness can lead to more thoughtful, compassionate digital citizenship, ultimately contributing to a more emotionally intelligent online community.

# Cultivating Compassion in Online Interactions

In the vast landscape of digital communication, cultivating compassion is not just a noble goal—it's a necessity for maintaining our humanity. As we navigate through social media platforms, online forums, and instant messaging apps, it's easy to forget that behind every username and profile picture is a real person with feelings, struggles, and aspirations. By consciously practicing empathy in our online interactions, we can create a more understanding and supportive digital environment that reflects the best of our human nature.

Developing digital compassion starts with a simple yet powerful shift in perspective. Before responding to a comment or post, take a moment to consider the person on the other end. What might they be going through? How could your words impact their day or even their life? This pause for reflection can transform potentially hurtful exchanges into opportunities for connection and growth. By choosing words that uplift rather than tear down, we contribute to a culture of kindness that can ripple far beyond our screens.

Practical steps towards fostering online compassion include actively listening (or in this case, carefully reading) before responding, offering support or encouragement when someone shares a struggle, and standing up against cyberbullying when we encounter it. Remember, every interaction is a chance to make the digital world a little bit brighter. As young digital citizens, you have the power to set the tone for online discourse and create spaces where empathy thrives. By doing so, you not only enhance your own online experiences but also contribute to a more compassionate digital future for everyone.

# Bridging the Empathy Gap: From Avatars to Real People

In our digital age, where screens mediate so many of our interactions, bridging the empathy gap between our online and offline lives has become crucial. As we navigate through a sea of avatars, usernames, and profile pictures, it's easy to forget that behind each digital representation is a real person with genuine emotions, struggles, and dreams. This disconnect can lead to a sense of detachment, making it challenging to form meaningful connections and truly understand the impact of our online actions on others.

To cultivate digital empathy, we must consciously remind ourselves of the humanity behind each online interaction. This means taking a moment to consider the person on the other side of the screen — their potential circumstances, feelings, and intentions. By doing so, we can begin to bridge the gap between the digital personas we encounter and the complex individuals they represent. Practicing this mindfulness not only enhances our online experiences but also helps us maintain our own humanity in an increasingly virtual world.

As young digital natives, you have the power to set a new standard for online interaction – one that prioritizes empathy, understanding, and respect. By treating online conversations with the same care and consideration you would give to face-to-face interactions, you can create a ripple effect of positivity in your digital communities. Remember, every comment, like, or share has the potential to impact someone's day, mood, or even life. By consciously connecting hearts through screens, you can help build a more compassionate and understanding digital landscape for everyone.

# Exercises for Developing Digital Empathy

Developing digital empathy is crucial in our increasingly connected world, and practicing it can lead to more meaningful online interactions. To cultivate this skill, start by actively listening to others in digital spaces, paying close attention to the emotions and intentions behind their words. Take a moment to consider how your messages might be interpreted before hitting send, and practice responding with kindness and understanding, even in challenging situations.

Another effective exercise for building digital empathy is to engage in perspective-taking. When encountering differing viewpoints online, challenge yourself to imagine the experiences and circumstances that might have shaped that person's opinion. This practice not only broadens your understanding but also fosters a more compassionate online environment. Additionally, seek out diverse voices and stories on social media platforms, actively following and engaging with people from different backgrounds to expand your digital empathy horizons.

Finally, remember that digital empathy extends beyond text-based interactions. When using video calls or voice chats, pay attention to non-verbal cues and tone of voice to better understand the emotions of others. Practice expressing your own feelings clearly and respectfully in these digital spaces. By consistently applying these exercises in your online interactions, you'll not only improve your digital empathy skills but also contribute to creating a more understanding and supportive digital world for everyone.

# CHAPTER 3

# ONLINE ETHICS: NAVIGATING THE VIRTUAL MORAL LANDSCAPE

# Navigating The Virtual Moral Landscape

Navigating the virtual moral landscape is a constant balancing act. It's about finding the line between free expression and responsible discourse, between personal privacy and the transparency of online interactions. It's about recognizing the potential for both good and harm in the digital realm, and making conscious choices that reflect our values and ethics. It's about being mindful of our online footprint, fostering empathy and understanding, and striving to create a virtual world that is both inclusive and respectful.

The virtual moral landscape is a complex tapestry woven with threads of anonymity, accessibility, and the constant evolution of technology. It requires us to be discerning consumers of information, to question narratives, and to critically evaluate the content we encounter. It's about holding ourselves and others accountable for our online actions, recognizing the impact of our words and deeds in the digital sphere. It's about navigating the gray areas, making ethical choices in the face of ambiguity, and contributing to a more positive and responsible online environment.

## The Influence of Social Media

Social media platforms have become powerful agents of change, influencing how young people form their values and understand the world. In the digital realm, the concept of "likes" and "followers" often trumps traditional values of respect and authenticity. The desire for validation and approval through social media can sometimes encourage behaviors that are more self-serving than altruistic. Self-promotion, comparison, and competition become driving forces, and in some cases, ethical considerations like honesty or privacy may take a backseat.

Moreover, the curated nature of social media—where users often present an idealized version of their lives—can create unrealistic expectations and foster feelings of inadequacy. The traditional value of humility, for instance, may be replaced by a culture of self-promotion, where appearances often matter more than substance.

## The Digital Age and Its Impact on the Traditional Morality of the Younger Generation

The advent of the digital age has brought about monumental changes in every aspect of our lives, from communication and education to entertainment and work. For the younger generation, who has grown up immersed in a world of technology, the digital age is not merely an external force but a foundational part of their identity. As this digital transformation continues to evolve, it is reshaping the traditional moral values that have long been passed down through generations.

Traditional morality is often grounded in communal values, cultural norms, and familial teachings. It has been shaped by religion, philosophy, and centuries of human experience. Concepts such as respect, honesty, empathy, responsibility, and integrity have been central to guiding behavior and fostering societal cohesion.

One of the defining characteristics of the digital age is the instant access to information, entertainment, and communication. The younger generation, accustomed to this rapid pace, may struggle with delayed gratification, which has long been a key principle of traditional morality. The digital age often rewards immediate results—whether it's getting an answer to a question in seconds or achieving social media fame in an instant—undermining the values of patience, perseverance, and long-term effort.

However, the digital age, with its boundless access to information and its global connectivity, is challenging these traditional notions of morality. The internet offers a platform where individuals can express themselves freely, but it also creates a space where the lines between right and wrong are not always clearly defined. For many young people, the digital world blurs these lines, leaving them to navigate a moral landscape that is not bound by the same principles that govern the offline world.

Despite these challenges, the digital age also provides an opportunity for the younger generation to redefine morality. With access to diverse perspectives and a wealth of global information, young people are exposed to different cultures, belief systems, and ways of thinking. This can lead to greater empathy and understanding, breaking down barriers and fostering a sense of shared humanity.

However, it requires a conscious effort to adapt traditional moral principles to the new reality. Values like respect, kindness, and honesty can still be upheld in the digital world, but they must be framed in a way that acknowledges the complexities of online interactions. The key is to encourage young people to think critically about the content they consume, the relationships they build, and the ethical implications of their actions in both the physical and digital realms.

# The Importance of Integrity in the Digital World

The digital age is reshaping the traditional morality of the younger generation in profound ways. While it presents new challenges—such as the erosion of privacy, the allure of instant gratification, and the impact of social media—it also offers opportunities for growth, connection, and redefinition. By embracing the values that have stood the test of time while adapting them to the realities of the digital world, the younger generation can forge a moral framework that is both timeless and relevant in the 21st century. The key lies in guiding young people to understand that technology should serve to enhance, not replace, the values that bind us together as a society.

In the digital age, integrity takes on new dimensions and challenges. As young people navigate the vast landscape of online interactions, maintaining one's moral compass becomes increasingly crucial. Integrity in the digital world means being true to oneself and one's values, even when hidden behind a screen or username. It involves making ethical choices, respecting others' privacy and rights, and taking responsibility for one's actions in virtual spaces just as one would in the physical world.

The anonymity and distance provided by digital platforms can sometimes tempt us to act in ways we wouldn't in face-to-face interactions. However, true integrity means consistency between our online and offline selves. It's about being honest in our communications, authentic in our self-presentation, and ethical in our use of information and technology. By cultivating digital integrity, we not only protect our own reputation and well-being but also contribute to creating a more trustworthy and positive online environment for all.

Practicing integrity in the digital world also means standing up for what's right, even when it's uncomfortable or unpopular. This could involve calling out cyberbullying, fact-checking before sharing information, or respecting intellectual property rights. By consciously choosing to act with integrity online, we strengthen our character, build meaningful digital relationships, and help shape a more ethical digital future. Remember, every online action, no matter how small, is a reflection of who we are and the world we want to create.

# Cyberbullying and Its Consequences

Cyberbullying has emerged as one of the most pressing challenges facing young people in the digital age. With the ubiquity of smartphones and social media platforms, bullying has transcended physical boundaries and can now occur 24/7, leaving victims feeling trapped and vulnerable even in their own homes. The anonymity provided by the internet often emboldens bullies, leading to more severe and persistent forms of harassment that can have devastating consequences on the mental health and well-being of those targeted affecting mental health, academic performance, and overall well-being. It is essential to understand the nature of cyberbullying and its far-reaching impacts in order to combat this growing issue.

The impact of cyberbullying extends far beyond the immediate emotional distress it causes. Victims often experience a range of long-term effects, including depression, anxiety, low self-esteem, and in extreme cases, suicidal thoughts. Moreover, the digital nature of cyberbullying means that hurtful messages or embarrassing content can be shared widely and persist online, potentially affecting a person's reputation and future opportunities. It's crucial for young people to understand the gravity of their online actions and the lasting damage they can inflict on others, even unintentionally.

Moreover, the anonymity that the digital world offers can lead to ethical dilemmas that challenge traditional notions of accountability. Cyberbullying, online harassment, and identity theft are issues that may not have been as prevalent in past generations. The ease with which people can engage in harmful behaviors without immediate consequences can desensitize young people to the real-world impact of their actions. The effects are evident in these three factors:

## 1. The Impact on Mental Health

The consequences of cyberbullying can be profound, particularly on the mental health of young people. Victims of cyberbullying may experience a range of emotional, psychological, and behavioral effects. The constant barrage of hurtful messages or the fear of being targeted online can lead to feelings of anxiety, depression, and loneliness. Victims often feel isolated and powerless, as they may not know where to turn for help.

- **Depression and Anxiety:** Repeated cyberbullying can lead to feelings of worthlessness and hopelessness, resulting in depression and anxiety. Victims may internalize the negative messages, believing that the harassment reflects their true worth. The emotional toll of cyberbullying can cause long-lasting psychological damage, affecting the individual's self-esteem and overall mental health.

- **Suicidal Thoughts:** In severe cases, cyberbullying can lead to thoughts of self-harm or suicide. Research has shown that cyberbullying is linked to a higher risk of suicidal ideation and attempts, particularly among adolescents. The pervasive nature of online bullying, combined with a lack of immediate support, can push vulnerable individuals into a crisis.

- **Social Withdrawal:** Victims of cyberbullying may become socially withdrawn, avoiding social interactions both online and offline. This withdrawal can lead to feelings of isolation and exacerbate mental health issues, creating a vicious cycle that is difficult to break.

2. **The Impact on Academic and Social Life**

Cyberbullying can also have significant consequences on a person's academic performance and social relationships. The emotional distress caused by cyberbullying can make it difficult for victims to concentrate on their studies, resulting in poor academic performance. They may struggle to focus in class, skip school, or avoid participating in activities due to feelings of anxiety or fear of being bullied online.

Socially, the effects of cyberbullying can lead to strained relationships with friends and family. Victims may become distrustful of others, particularly online friends, leading to social isolation. They may also become less willing to participate in online communities or social media platforms due to the fear of further harassment. This withdrawal can prevent them from forming meaningful connections and support networks.

## 3. Legal and Social Consequences

Cyberbullying doesn't just have emotional and social consequences—it can also lead to legal repercussions. In many jurisdictions, cyberbullying is considered a criminal offense. Perpetrators of cyberbullying may face charges related to harassment, defamation, or even identity theft, depending on the severity of the actions. Laws are evolving to address the rise of cyberbullying, with many countries now implementing stricter regulations to hold offenders accountable.

In addition to legal consequences, cyberbullying can lead to reputational damage for the perpetrator. If a bully is identified, they may face public backlash, social ostracism, and even damage to their future academic or career prospects. The consequences of their actions may extend far beyond the immediate victim, affecting their own lives and the lives of those around them.

# Combating Cyberbullying

Combating cyberbullying requires a multi-faceted approach involving education, empathy, and proactive measures. By fostering digital empathy and promoting responsible online behavior, we can create a more compassionate virtual environment. It's essential for young people to learn how to recognize cyberbullying, support those who are targeted, and stand up against online harassment. Additionally, understanding how to use privacy settings, report abusive behavior, and seek help from trusted adults or online support services can empower individuals to protect themselves and others in the digital realm.

Schools, parents, and communities can play a crucial role in preventing and addressing cyberbullying by:

1. **Raising Awareness:** Educating children, teenagers, and adults about the harmful effects of cyberbullying and how to recognize and report it.

2. **Providing Support:** Offering resources for victims of cyberbullying, including counseling, peer support groups, and safe spaces where they can talk about their experiences.

3. **Encouraging Positive Online Behavior:** Teaching individuals how to engage respectfully online and use digital platforms responsibly.

4. **Legal Action and Reporting:** Encouraging victims to report cyberbullying to authorities and utilizing legal avenues to hold perpetrators accountable.

Social media platforms and digital companies must also play a more active role in combatting cyberbullying. By implementing stricter reporting systems, better content moderation, and providing resources for users who may be experiencing harassment, these platforms can help create safer online environments.

# The Nature of Cyberbullying

Cyberbullying can take many forms, including but not limited to:

1. **Harassment:** Repeatedly sending offensive, threatening, or hurtful messages to an individual.

2. **Doxing:** Publicly revealing private information about someone, such as their

home address, phone number, or other personal details, with the intention of causing harm.

3. **Exclusion:** Deliberately excluding someone from an online group, chat, or activity to cause feelings of isolation and rejection.

4. **Impersonation:** Creating fake profiles or accounts to impersonate someone, spreading false or damaging information to harm their reputation.

5. **Cyberstalking:** Using digital platforms to harass or stalk someone persistently, often leading to fear for personal safety.

6. **Outing:** Sharing private or embarrassing information, images, or videos about someone without their consent.

One of the key characteristics of cyberbullying is its ability to reach victims anywhere, anytime. Unlike traditional bullying, which usually takes place within specific environments such as schools or neighborhoods, cyberbullying can invade the privacy of a person's home. This constant access to the victim, coupled with the fact that many social media platforms allow individuals to remain anonymous, can make it difficult to escape the harassment.

## Privacy, Security, and Responsible Data Sharing

In our increasingly interconnected digital world, privacy and security have become paramount concerns for young people navigating online spaces. As we share more of our lives on social media platforms, messaging apps, and various online services, it's crucial to understand the implications of our digital footprint. This section will explore the delicate balance between staying connected and protecting your personal information, offering practical strategies to safeguard your online presence while still enjoying the benefits of the digital age.

Responsible data sharing is a skill that every digital native must master. It's not just about protecting yourself; it's about respecting the privacy and security of others as well. We'll delve into the ethical considerations of sharing information online, from the seemingly innocuous act of tagging friends in photos to the more complex issues of data ownership and consent. By developing a thoughtful approach to data sharing, you can contribute to a safer, more respectful online environment for everyone.

As we navigate this complex landscape, it's important to remember that privacy and security are not just personal matters — they have broader implications for society as a whole. We'll examine how individual choices in data sharing can impact communities, influence public discourse, and shape the future of digital interactions. By cultivating a mindset of responsible digital citizenship, you can play a vital role in creating a more ethical and secure online world for generations to come.

# Ethical Decision-Making in Online Environments

In the digital age, ethical decision-making has become increasingly complex, especially for young people navigating online environments. The virtual world presents unique challenges that often blur the lines between right and wrong, making it crucial for teenagers and young adults to develop a strong moral compass. As we interact with others through screens and keyboards, it's easy to forget that our actions have real-world consequences, affecting both ourselves and those around us.

To make ethical decisions online, it's essential to cultivate digital empathy – the ability to understand and share the feelings of others in virtual spaces. This means considering the impact of our words and actions on real people, even when we can't see their immediate reactions. By pausing to reflect before posting, commenting, or sharing content, we can ensure that our online behavior aligns with our values and contributes positively to the digital community.

Developing a framework for ethical decision-making in online environments is crucial for maintaining our humanity in the digital age. This involves asking ourselves important questions: Does this action reflect my true self and values? Would I be comfortable with this decision if it were made public? How might this affect others, both now and in the future? By consistently applying these ethical considerations to our online interactions, we can create a more respectful, compassionate, and responsible digital world that enhances rather than diminishes our human connections.

# CHAPTER 4

# THE POWER OF FACE-TO-FACE CONNECTIONS

# The Power of Face-to-Face Connections

The power of face-to-face connections lies in the irreplaceable human touch. It's the warmth of a smile, the depth of a shared glance, the subtle nuances of body language that can't be replicated through a screen. It's the energy of a conversation where laughter echoes in the room, where empathy flows freely, and where genuine understanding blossoms. It's the magic of human interaction, where shared experiences forge bonds that transcend words, creating connections that are both profound and enduring.

One of the most powerful aspects of face-to-face communication is the ability to build stronger, more meaningful relationships. When people meet in person, they can connect not just through words but through non-verbal cues—body language, facial expressions, tone of voice—which provide additional layers of understanding. These subtle, yet significant, elements help create a more authentic connection, allowing individuals to read between the lines and gauge emotions and intentions in ways that are harder to achieve through digital means.

In professional settings, face-to-face meetings help build trust and rapport. In-person interactions are often more personal, allowing for genuine exchanges that lead to stronger working relationships. Whether it's a handshake, a smile, or a shared experience in the same physical space, these small gestures foster connection and trust in ways that emails and messages can't match.

# Rediscovering the Value of In-Person Interactions

In our increasingly digital world, it's easy to forget the irreplaceable value of face-to-face interactions. As we navigate through a sea of screens and virtual connections, we risk losing touch with the fundamental human need for physical presence and genuine, in-person communication. This section explores why rediscovering and prioritizing real-world interactions is crucial for maintaining our humanity and fostering meaningful relationships in the digital age.

The power of in-person connections lies in their ability to engage all our senses and emotions in ways that digital interactions simply cannot replicate. When we meet face-to-face, we pick up on subtle cues like body language, facial expressions, and tone of voice that are often lost in text messages or video calls. These nonverbal elements of communication play a vital role in building trust, empathy, and understanding between individuals. By consciously seeking out and valuing these in-person interactions, we can deepen our connections and enrich our social experiences in ways that technology alone cannot achieve.

For young people growing up in a hyper-connected digital landscape, it's especially important to recognize the unique benefits of real-world interactions. Face-to-face conversations and shared experiences create lasting memories and bonds that form the foundation of strong friendships and communities. They also provide opportunities for personal growth, as we learn to navigate social situations, read emotions, and develop crucial interpersonal skills. By balancing our online presence with meaningful offline connections, we can harness the best of both worlds and cultivate a more fulfilling and well-rounded social life.

## Balancing Online and Offline Relationships

In today's digital age, striking a balance between online and offline relationships has become increasingly crucial, especially for young adults navigating the complexities of social interactions. While technology offers unprecedented connectivity, it's essential to recognize the unique value of face-to-face connections in fostering deeper, more meaningful relationships. The challenge lies in leveraging the benefits of digital communication without sacrificing the richness of in-person interactions that are fundamental to our social and emotional well-being.

To achieve this balance, it's important to be mindful of how we allocate our time and attention between virtual and physical spaces. Set boundaries for your online activities, designating specific times for social media and messaging, while also prioritizing face-to-face meetups with friends and family. Engage in activities that encourage personal interaction, such as joining clubs, participating in team sports, or volunteering in your community. These experiences not only enrich your social life but also help develop crucial interpersonal skills that may be underutilized in purely digital communications.

Remember that quality trumps quantity when it comes to relationships. While you might have hundreds of online connections, focus on nurturing a core group of meaningful relationships both online and offline. Make an effort to translate digital friendships into real-world connections when possible, and don't shy away from vulnerable, honest conversations that are often easier to have in person. By consciously balancing your online and offline interactions, you'll create a more fulfilling social life that harnesses the best of both worlds, ensuring that technology enhances rather than replaces the irreplaceable human element in your relationships.

## Techniques for Meaningful Face-to-Face Communication

In an era dominated by digital communication, mastering the art of meaningful face-to-face interaction has become more crucial than ever. As young adults navigating the complexities of the digital age, it's essential to cultivate techniques that foster genuine connections in person. By honing these skills, you can create deeper relationships, build empathy, and maintain a strong sense of humanity in your daily interactions.

One key technique for meaningful face-to-face communication is active listening. This involves giving your full attention to the person speaking, maintaining eye contact, and responding with thoughtful questions or comments. By practicing active listening, you demonstrate respect for others' perspectives and create an environment where authentic dialogue can flourish. Additionally, being mindful of your body language and facial expressions can significantly enhance your ability to connect with others on a more profound level.

Another powerful technique is to practice vulnerability and authenticity in your conversations. While it may feel uncomfortable at first, sharing your genuine thoughts and feelings can lead to more meaningful and memorable interactions. By being open and honest, you invite others to do the same, creating a space for mutual understanding and growth. Remember, true connection often happens when we move beyond surface-level small talk and engage in conversations that matter, allowing our shared humanity to shine through even in a world increasingly mediated by screens.

## Creating Tech-Free Zones and Moments

In our hyper-connected world, it's crucial to create intentional spaces and moments free from the constant buzz of technology. These tech-free zones serve as sanctuaries where we can reconnect with ourselves, our loved ones, and the physical world around us. By designating specific areas in our homes, such as the dining room or bedroom, as device-free zones, we create opportunities for genuine face-to-face interactions and undistracted relaxation.

Similarly, carving out tech-free moments throughout our day can have a profound impact on our well-being and relationships. This could be as simple as taking a daily walk without your phone, engaging in a hobby without digital distractions, or implementing a 'no phones at the table' rule during meals. These deliberate pauses from the digital world allow us to practice mindfulness, improve our focus, and cultivate deeper connections with those around us. This is referred to as a "**Digital Detox**", a practice that encourages us to disconnect from the constant flow of information and reconnect with ourselves and the real world.

As you navigate the digital age, challenge yourself to gradually increase these tech-free zones and moments in your life. Start small, perhaps with a 30-minute device-free period each day, and observe how it affects your mood, productivity, and relationships. Remember, the goal isn't to completely disconnect from technology, but to strike a healthy balance that allows you to fully embrace both the digital and physical aspects of your life. By creating these intentional spaces and moments, you're taking a significant step towards preserving your humanity in our increasingly digital world.

# The Paradox of Digital Relationships

In a world where technology is seamlessly woven into the fabric of daily life, we find ourselves constantly connected, yet increasingly distant. The advent of the digital age has revolutionized how we communicate, allowing us to bridge vast distances and share experiences in real-time. Through screens, we can connect with friends, family, and even strangers across the globe, forging relationships that transcend physical boundaries. But as we grow more connected digitally, we must ask: Are these connections truly enriching our lives, or are they leaving us longing for deeper, more authentic human interaction?

The digital era has brought people closer in ways once unimaginable. Social media platforms, messaging apps, and video calls enable us to share moments, emotions, and milestones with those we love, no matter where they are in the world. In an instant, we can celebrate a friend's birthday, comfort a family member during a difficult time, or even meet new people with similar passions and interests. These connections—often facilitated through screens—have made the world feel smaller and more interconnected.

Moreover, technology has given a voice to the voiceless, providing a platform for individuals to share their stories and connect with others who understand their struggles and triumphs. This can create a sense of belonging and community, offering solace to those who may feel isolated or unheard in their immediate surroundings.

Despite these advancements, there is a growing recognition that the digital age is not without its contradictions. For all the convenience and speed of communication, digital connections can sometimes feel hollow and superficial. The act of sending a text, liking a post, or commenting on a photo lacks the emotional depth of a face-to-face conversation or a handwritten letter. Words on a screen may convey information, but they do not always capture the nuances of tone, body language, or unspoken emotion that are integral to human connection.

Moreover, the constant stream of notifications and digital distractions can create a paradox of connection: We are connected to more people than ever before, yet many of us feel lonelier than ever. Social media, for example, can encourage comparison and competition, where curated lives and filtered images often mask the realities of everyday struggles. This can lead to feelings of inadequacy or disconnection, as people struggle to measure up to the carefully constructed personas of others.

While digital platforms provide a convenient means of staying in touch, they cannot replace the depth and richness of face-to-face interactions. True emotional connection arises not just from words exchanged through screens but from shared experiences, physical presence, and the bond that forms when we are fully engaged with one another in real time.

In a world of constant digital interaction, it is important to find balance. Technology should be viewed as a tool—one that can enhance our connections but not replace the importance of genuine human contact. The challenge lies in finding ways to connect meaningfully through screens while maintaining the authenticity and emotional depth of traditional relationships.

To truly connect hearts through screens, we must be intentional in how we use technology. This means engaging in deeper conversations, being present when interacting with others, and cultivating online spaces that encourage empathy, vulnerability, and authenticity. We can use digital tools to amplify meaningful interactions, not just for convenience, but to create lasting bonds.

We can also prioritize in-person connections, ensuring that digital relationships are complemented by moments of face-to-face engagement. Whether it's sharing a meal, going for a walk, or simply sitting together in silence, these real-world moments are essential in nurturing the depth of connection that technology alone cannot provide.

# CHAPTER 5

# HARNESSING TECHNOLOGY FOR PERSONAL GROWTH

# Harnessing Technology for Personal Growth

Harnessing technology for personal growth is a delicate dance between embracing its potential and avoiding its pitfalls. It's about recognizing that technology is a powerful tool, capable of both amplifying our strengths and exacerbating our weaknesses.

The key lies in conscious intentionality. We must choose to use technology in a way that aligns with our values and goals. This means actively seeking out resources that support our personal development, whether it's online courses, meditation apps, or platforms that connect us with like-minded individuals. It also means setting boundaries, prioritizing real-world experiences, and resisting the allure of constant digital stimulation.

Technology can be a powerful catalyst for self-discovery. It can open doors to new knowledge, connect us with mentors and communities, and provide tools for self-reflection and mindfulness.

However, it's crucial to remember that technology is a means to an end, not an end in itself. We must use it strategically, ensuring that it serves our personal growth journey rather than hindering it.

Ultimately, harnessing technology for personal growth requires a mindful approach. It's about being aware of our digital habits, making conscious choices, and using technology as a tool to empower ourselves, expand our horizons, and live a more fulfilling life.

# Using Digital Tools for Self-Reflection and Mindfulness

In our fast-paced digital world, it's easy to get caught up in the constant stream of information and notifications. However, the same technology that can overwhelm us also offers powerful tools for self-reflection and mindfulness. By leveraging digital apps and platforms designed for meditation, journaling, and mood tracking, young people can cultivate a deeper understanding of themselves and their emotions. These tools provide structured ways to pause, reflect, and reconnect with our inner selves, even in the midst of our busy digital lives.

One of the most effective ways to use technology for self-reflection is through digital journaling apps. These platforms offer prompts, mood trackers, and the ability to add photos or voice notes, making it easier than ever to document our thoughts and feelings. By consistently recording our experiences and emotions, we can identify patterns in our behavior, recognize triggers for stress or anxiety, and celebrate our personal growth over time. This digital form of introspection can be particularly appealing to tech-savvy teenagers and young adults, providing a familiar and accessible medium for self-discovery.

Mindfulness apps have also revolutionized the way we approach mental well-being in the digital age. With guided meditations, breathing exercises, and even virtual reality relaxation experiences, these tools make it possible to create moments of calm and presence throughout our day. By incorporating these digital mindfulness practices into our routines, we can develop greater emotional resilience, improve our focus, and cultivate a sense of inner peace. As we navigate the complexities of the online world, these digital tools for self-reflection and mindfulness serve as a compass, helping us stay grounded in our values and connected to our humanity.

## Online Learning and Skill Development

In the digital age, online learning has revolutionized the way we acquire knowledge and develop new skills. For young people navigating this landscape, the internet offers an unprecedented wealth of resources, from free courses on platforms like Coursera and edX to specialized tutorials on YouTube. The internet has opened up a world of learning opportunities. Take online courses, read blogs and articles, and explore new topics that interest you.

This democratization of education has opened doors for self-directed learning, allowing individuals to pursue their passions and enhance their abilities at their own pace.

However, the abundance of online learning opportunities also presents challenges. With so many options available, it's crucial to develop discernment and critical thinking skills to identify quality resources and avoid misinformation. Additionally, the self-discipline required for online learning can be a hurdle for some, as the lack of structure and face-to-face interaction may lead to procrastination or incomplete learning experiences.

To truly harness the power of online learning, it's essential to approach it with intention and balance. Set clear goals, create a structured learning schedule, and seek out ways to apply your new knowledge in real-world contexts. Remember that while online resources are invaluable, they should complement, not replace, traditional forms of education and hands-on experience. By thoughtfully integrating online learning into your personal growth journey, you can cultivate a lifelong love for learning and continuously adapt to our ever-changing digital world.

# Building Positive Digital Communities

In the vast landscape of the digital world, building positive online communities has become more crucial than ever for young people. These virtual spaces, when nurtured with care and intention, can become powerful platforms for connection, support, and personal growth. By actively participating in and contributing to positive digital communities, teenagers and young adults can create environments that reflect their values, foster meaningful relationships, and promote collective well-being.

To build and maintain these positive digital spaces, it's essential to practice digital empathy and online ethics. This means being mindful of how our words and actions impact others, even when we can't see their immediate reactions. Encourage respectful dialogue, celebrate diversity, and stand up against cyberbullying or hate speech. By doing so, you not only contribute to a healthier online ecosystem but also develop valuable skills in communication, leadership, and conflict resolution that will serve you well both online and offline.

Remember that positive digital communities don't exist in isolation from the real world. They can be powerful catalysts for offline action and change. Use these online spaces to organize events, collaborate on projects, or rally support for causes you care about. By bridging the gap between digital and physical interactions, you can harness the full potential of technology to create meaningful connections and drive positive change in your local communities and beyond. In doing so, you'll be actively shaping a more compassionate, balanced, and fulfilling world for yourself and future generations.

# Technology as a Catalyst for Social Change

In the digital age, technology has emerged as a powerful catalyst for social change, offering unprecedented opportunities for young people to make a difference in the world. Social media platforms, mobile apps, and online communities have become virtual town squares where ideas spread rapidly, movements gain momentum, and collective action takes shape. From raising awareness about global issues to organizing grassroots campaigns, technology empowers teenagers and young adults to amplify their voices and effect change on a scale previously unimaginable.

However, with this power comes the responsibility to use technology ethically and thoughtfully. As digital natives, young people must learn to navigate the complexities of online activism, distinguishing between meaningful engagement and performative 'slacktivism.' It's crucial to understand that while technology can be a powerful tool for social change, it should complement rather than replace real-world actions and face-to-face interactions. By striking a balance between digital advocacy and tangible, local efforts, young changemakers can harness the full potential of technology to create lasting, positive impact in their communities and beyond.

Moreover, technology's role in social change extends beyond activism to innovation and problem-solving. Crowdfunding platforms enable young entrepreneurs to bring socially conscious ideas to life, while open-source collaboration allows for the rapid development of solutions to global challenges. As we navigate this digital landscape, it's essential to approach technology not just as consumers, but as creators and innovators. By embracing this mindset, young people can leverage technology to address social issues, bridge divides, and shape a more equitable and sustainable future. The key lies in using our digital tools with intention, empathy, and a clear vision of the positive change we wish to see in the world.

# CHAPTER 6

# CHARTING YOUR COURSE: CREATING A BALANCE LIFE

# Creating A Balance Life

Creating a balanced life in the digital age is a constant dance between embracing technology's benefits and guarding against its potential dangers. It's about finding a rhythm that allows us to thrive in both the physical and digital worlds, without letting one dominate the other.

The first step is to recognize the subtle ways technology can creep into our lives, subtly influencing our thoughts, emotions, and behaviors. We must be mindful of our digital consumption, setting boundaries around screen time, and prioritizing real-world experiences. This might mean disconnecting for a designated period each day, engaging in activities that don't involve screens, or simply being more present in the moment.

Cultivating a balanced life also involves redefining our relationship with technology. Instead of viewing it as a constant source of entertainment or distraction, we can harness its power for personal growth and meaningful connections. This could involve using technology for learning, connecting with loved ones, or pursuing creative passions.

Ultimately, creating a balanced life in the digital age is about prioritizing well-being. It's about ensuring that technology enhances our lives, rather than detracts from them. It's about finding a rhythm that allows us to thrive in both the physical and digital worlds, embracing the best of both while mitigating the potential downsides.

# Developing a Personal Technology Philosophy

In today's digital landscape, developing a personal technology philosophy is crucial for maintaining a balanced and fulfilling life. This philosophy serves as your compass, guiding your interactions with digital devices and online platforms while ensuring that technology enhances rather than detracts from your human experience. By consciously crafting your approach to technology use, you create a framework that aligns with your values, goals, and the person you aspire to be in both the digital and physical worlds.

To develop your personal technology philosophy, start by reflecting on your current relationship with digital devices and online platforms. Consider how technology impacts your daily life, relationships, and overall well-being. Ask yourself thought-provoking questions: Does your current tech usage align with your personal values? Are you using digital tools to enhance your productivity and creativity, or do they sometimes hinder your progress? By critically examining your digital habits, you can identify areas where technology serves you well and where it may be detracting from your quality of life.

Once you've gained clarity on your current tech habits, envision the ideal role of technology in your life. This vision should encompass how you want to engage with digital platforms, manage your online presence, and balance screen time with offline activities. Your personal technology philosophy might include principles such as prioritizing face-to-face interactions, setting boundaries for device usage, or using technology intentionally to pursue personal growth and meaningful connections. Remember, this philosophy is uniquely yours – it should reflect your individual needs, aspirations, and the values that guide you in navigating the complex digital landscape of our time.

# Setting Boundaries and Managing Screen Time

In our hyper-connected world, setting boundaries and managing screen time have become essential skills for maintaining a balanced digital life. As young adults, you're constantly bombarded with notifications, messages, and the allure of endless scrolling, making it challenging to disconnect and focus on real-world experiences. However, by establishing clear boundaries and implementing effective screen time management strategies, you can regain control over your digital consumption and create space for personal growth, face-to-face relationships, and offline pursuits.

To begin setting boundaries, start by identifying your priorities and values. Reflect on what truly matters to you – whether it's spending quality time with loved ones, pursuing hobbies, or focusing on your studies – and allocate your time accordingly. Create designated 'tech-free' zones or periods in your day, such as during meals, before bedtime, or while engaging in meaningful conversations. By doing so, you're not only reducing your screen time but also cultivating mindfulness and presence in your daily life.

Managing screen time effectively doesn't mean completely eliminating technology from your life; rather, it's about finding a healthy balance. Utilize built-in tools on your devices or download apps that track and limit your screen time. Set realistic goals for reducing your digital consumption, and gradually work towards them. Remember, the aim is to use technology intentionally and purposefully, rather than mindlessly. By mastering the art of setting boundaries and managing your screen time, you'll be better equipped to navigate the digital landscape while staying true to your human essence and values.

# Cultivating Authentic Self-Expression Online

In the digital age, authentic self-expression has become both a challenge and an opportunity for young people. Social media platforms offer unprecedented avenues for sharing our thoughts, feelings, and experiences with the world. However, the pressure to present a curated, 'perfect' version of ourselves online can often lead to a disconnect between our digital personas and our true selves. As we navigate this complex landscape, it's crucial to remember that genuine self-expression is not about conforming to online trends or seeking validation through likes and shares, but rather about staying true to our values, passions, and unique perspectives.

Cultivating authentic self-expression online requires a delicate balance between openness and boundaries. It's about sharing aspects of our lives that reflect our true selves while also maintaining a sense of privacy and personal space. This might mean being selective about the content we post, focusing on quality over quantity, and engaging in meaningful conversations rather than surface-level interactions. By approaching our online presence with intention and mindfulness, we can create digital spaces that nurture our individuality and foster genuine connections with others.

Remember, your online presence is an extension of your real-world self, not a separate entity. Strive to align your digital footprint with your personal values and goals. This alignment not only helps in maintaining authenticity but also contributes to a more fulfilling and balanced digital life. By embracing your unique voice and perspective, you can inspire others to do the same, creating a ripple effect of authenticity in the digital world. In doing so, we collectively work towards a more genuine, empathetic, and human-centered online environment.

# Becoming Digital Citizens and Future Leaders

As we navigate the digital landscape, it's crucial for young people to recognize their role as digital citizens and future leaders. The choices we make online today shape not only our personal experiences but also the collective digital environment we inhabit. By cultivating digital empathy, practicing responsible online behavior, and understanding the far-reaching consequences of our virtual actions, we can become positive forces in the digital world.

To become effective digital citizens, we must first develop a strong sense of ethics that transcends the boundaries between our online and offline lives. This means treating others with respect in digital spaces, protecting our own and others' privacy, and using technology as a tool for positive change. By doing so, we lay the foundation for responsible leadership in an increasingly interconnected world, where the lines between physical and digital realities continue to blur.

As future leaders, it's essential to harness the power of technology while staying grounded in our humanity. This involves striking a balance between leveraging digital tools for innovation and progress, and nurturing face-to-face connections that foster deep understanding and empathy. By embracing this dual approach, we can lead by example, showing others how to thrive in the digital age without losing touch with the core values that make us human. In doing so, we pave the way for a more compassionate, ethical, and balanced digital future.

# CHAPTER 7

# THE FUTURE WITH Ai: SHAPING THE WORLD OF TOMMOROW

# Shaping the World of Tomorrow with Ai

Artificial Intelligence (Ai) is rapidly transforming our world, permeating industries, revolutionizing economies, and reshaping how we live, work, and interact. As we stand on the brink of an Ai-driven future, the possibilities are immense, and the challenges are equally profound. Understanding AI's potential and preparing for its implications is critical to harnessing its benefits responsibly and ethically.

## The Current State of Ai

Ai is already an integral part of our lives, from virtual assistants like Siri and Alexa to recommendation algorithms powering platforms like Netflix and Amazon. In healthcare, AI aids in diagnosing diseases and predicting patient outcomes. In transportation, self-driving cars are becoming a reality. Industries are using Ai to automate processes, improve efficiency, and analyze massive datasets. These advancements showcase Ai's capability to enhance productivity, reduce costs, and create innovative solutions to complex problems.

Artificial Intelligence has transitioned from a speculative concept to a central force driving technological advancement across the globe. Over the past few years, we've witnessed Ai's rapid growth and integration into various sectors— healthcare, finance, retail, and more. While we are still in the early stages of AI's potential, the current state of AI reveals both impressive capabilities and significant challenges that need to be addressed as the technology evolves.

Today, Ai is a combination of machine learning, deep learning, natural language processing, computer vision, and robotics, all of which enable machines to perform tasks that typically require human intelligence. Machine learning (ML), in particular, has made tremendous strides. By training algorithms on vast amounts of data, Ai systems can recognize patterns, make predictions, and improve over time.

Natural Language Processing (NLP), one of the most rapidly advancing areas of Ai allows machines to understand, interpret, and generate human language. Tools like chatbots, virtual assistants (such as Siri and Alexa), and machine translation systems have already become integral parts of our daily lives. In addition, Ai-driven systems are now capable of conducting sophisticated conversations, generating human-like text, and even writing articles, making it clear that NLP has moved beyond its infancy.

Another significant development is computer vision, which allows Ai systems to process and analyze visual data, enabling applications such as facial recognition, object detection, and autonomous vehicles. The current state of Ai is marked by increasing precision in these areas, helping improve security, manufacturing, and other industries that rely on visual input.

# The Promising Future of Ai

The future of Ai is brimming with possibilities. Advancements in machine learning, natural language processing, and robotics are paving the way for unprecedented innovations:

### 1. The Rise of Ai: A Revolution in Technology

Ai, at its core, refers to the development of machines and systems that can perform tasks typically requiring human intelligence. These tasks include problem-solving, decision-making, language understanding, and pattern recognition. The applications of Ai are vast, ranging from self-driving cars and virtual assistants to advanced medical diagnostics and Ai-powered robots. With the help of machine learning, AI can process vast amounts of data, learn from it, and improve its performance over time—enabling it to adapt and solve complex challenges in ways that were once unimaginable.

As Ai becomes increasingly integrated into our daily lives, it is not just enhancing existing technologies but is also creating entirely new industries. Fields like robotics, natural language processing, and predictive analytics are growing exponentially, opening up new opportunities for innovation. The future promises even more breakthroughs, with AI potentially advancing to the point where it can independently think, create, and drive entire sectors of the economy.

## 2. Ai in Healthcare: A New Era of Medicine

One of the most promising areas where Ai is poised to shape the world of tomorrow is healthcare. Ai's ability to analyze massive datasets quickly and accurately is already being used to improve diagnostics, develop personalized treatment plans, and even predict potential health risks before they occur. Algorithms that analyze medical images, such as MRIs and X-rays, can identify patterns that might be missed by human eyes, enabling early detection of diseases like cancer, heart conditions, and neurological disorders.

Additionally, Ai-powered robots are assisting surgeons in performing complex procedures with greater precision, reducing recovery times, and minimizing the risk of complications. The integration of Ai in drug discovery is also accelerating the development of new treatments, allowing scientists to identify potential drug candidates in record time. As Ai continues to evolve, the dream of more efficient, accessible, and personalized healthcare is within reach.

### 3. Education: Redefining Learning and Access

In education, Ai has the potential to revolutionize how we learn, teach, and access knowledge. Ai-driven tools are already being used to create personalized learning experiences, tailoring educational content to individual students' needs, learning styles, and progress. This individualized approach can help students learn at their own pace, improving engagement and outcomes.

Moreover, Ai can break down geographical and financial barriers to education. Online learning platforms powered by Ai can offer high-quality education to people in remote or underserved areas, democratizing access to knowledge and creating new opportunities for self-improvement. Ai can also assist teachers by automating administrative tasks, allowing them to focus more on pedagogy and student interaction.

### 4. Business and Automation: Efficiency and Innovation

In the business world, Ai is driving innovation and efficiency across industries. From automating routine tasks to enhancing customer service with chatbots, Ai is helping companies streamline operations, reduce costs, and improve productivity. Machine learning algorithms are also being used to analyze consumer behavior, predict trends, and personalize marketing strategies, enabling businesses to provide more relevant and targeted services.

However, Ai's impact on the workforce cannot be ignored. As automation takes over repetitive tasks, there will be a need for workers to adapt and acquire new skills in areas like Ai programming, data analysis, and machine learning. The future of work will likely see an increased demand for highly skilled workers who can collaborate with Ai systems and drive innovation in tandem with automation.

## Ethical Challenges and Risks

Despite its promise, Ai poses significant ethical challenges. The potential for bias in AI systems, stemming from biased training data, raises concerns about fairness and discrimination. Privacy issues are another major concern, as Ai systems collect and analyze vast amounts of personal data. Moreover, the automation of jobs could lead to widespread unemployment, necessitating the re-skilling of workers and rethinking economic systems.

There are also fears about Ai's misuse, such as in the development of autonomous weapons or surveillance systems that infringe on civil liberties. Addressing these challenges requires robust ethical frameworks, transparent Ai development, and global cooperation.

# Preparing for an Ai-Driven World

To ensure Ai benefits humanity, collaboration between governments, industries, and academia is essential. Policies and regulations must be designed to promote fairness, transparency, and accountability in Ai systems. Investing in education and training programs will prepare the workforce for the jobs of the future.

Individuals, too, have a role to play. Developing digital literacy and critical thinking skills will help people navigate the Ai-driven world responsibly.

The future is undeniably intertwined with Ai, and the potential for positive change is enormous. From revolutionizing healthcare and education to driving economic growth and innovation, Ai has the power to shape a world that is more efficient, equitable, and connected. However, as we move forward, it is important to navigate the challenges that come with this technology, ensuring that Ai serves humanity's best interests and adheres to ethical standards. By fostering collaboration between technologists, policymakers, and society, we can create a future where Ai enhances human potential, enriches lives, and addresses the world's most pressing problems. The world of tomorrow, shaped by Ai, holds limitless possibilities—if we approach it with foresight, responsibility, and a commitment to the greater good.

# EPILOGUE

As we stand at the crossroads of human history, the digital age emerges as a defining chapter, one that has redefined the very fabric of our existence. It is an era of boundless opportunities and unforeseen challenges, where technology serves as both a beacon of progress and a mirror reflecting our deepest aspirations and vulnerabilities.

The digital age has connected the world in ways once thought impossible. It has brought people, cultures, and ideas closer together, fostering innovation and driving human advancement. Knowledge, once confined to the privileged few, is now accessible to anyone with an internet connection. From the humblest homes to the grandest institutions, the digital revolution has become a force that shapes our dreams and ambitions.

Yet, this era is not without its shadows. The relentless pace of technological advancement has raised questions about identity, privacy, and ethics.

The promise of connectivity sometimes isolates, as we lose ourselves in virtual worlds and curated realities. The convenience of automation challenges the essence of what it means to work, create, and belong.

In this brave new world, the tools we have created reflect not only our ingenuity but also our humanity—our capacity for both great good and profound harm. The digital age holds a mirror to society, revealing our potential while demanding accountability. It calls for balance: between innovation and tradition, between individuality and community, between the digital and the tangible.

As we navigate this transformative era, let us remember that technology is a tool, not an identity. It should serve as a means to enhance our lives, not define them. The digital age is not merely about screens and circuits; it is about the choices we make and the values we uphold.

The future is unwritten, and the digital age is but one chapter in humanity's ongoing story. It is up to us to decide how this chapter will be remembered—whether as a time when we were consumed by the machines we created or as an era where we harnessed their power to uplift and unite.

In the end, the digital age is not an endpoint but a beginning. It is an opportunity to redefine what it means to be human in a world of infinite possibilities. Let us seize this moment with wisdom, courage, and hope, ensuring that our digital legacy is one of progress, purpose, and profound connection.

## ABOUT THE AUTHOR

Ray Smith is a visionary author and social observer with a passion for inspiring positive change in young people. With a background in corporate supervision and people management, Smith has dedicated his career to exploring the delicate balance between technological advancement and human values. His unique perspective and engaging writing style make him the perfect guide for young readers navigating the complexities of the modern world. Additionally, he works in the book publishing industry as a Book Growth Specialist, a field significantly impacted by advancements in AI.